THE LITTLE GIANT BOOK OF

OPTICAL
Tricks

Keith Kay

Sterling Publishing Co., Inc.
New York

10 9 8 7 6 5 4 3 2

Published by Sterling Publishing Company, Inc.
387 Park Avenue South, New York, N.Y. 10016
© 2000 by Keith Kay
Distributed in Canada by Sterling Publishing
c/o Canadian Manda Group, One Atlantic Avenue, Suite 105
Toronto, Ontario, Canada M6K 3E7
Distributed in Great Britain and Europe by Cassell PLC
Wellington House, 125 Strand, London WC2R 0BB, England
Distributed in Australia by Capricorn Link (Australia) Pty Ltd.
P.O. Box 6651, Baulkham Hills, Business Centre, NSW 2153,
Australia
Manufactured in the United States of America

Sterling ISBN 0-8069-0252-3

HELLO

Welcome to *The Little Giant Book of Optical Tricks*. This book contains a great collection of visual pictures, puzzles, and oddities.

After I had compiled the first book, *The Little Giant Book of Optical Illusions*, I didn't think there would be enough material for a second volume. But how wrong can you be? I am grateful to all the people who have offered help and suggestions.

This book contains lots of "variations" on a theme, which adds to the enjoyment of a fascinating subject. Lots of the pictures haven't been seen in print for many years, some are "reflections on a bygone age."

I hope you will enjoy this book. It will prove again that seeing is sometimes deceiving!

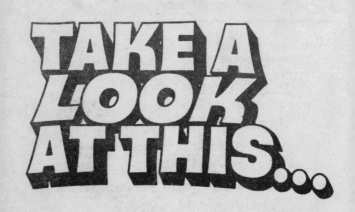

Answers are in the back of the book.

Which of these two boys has the wider mouth, A or B?

Do you notice anything unusual about the
way the word "honey" has been written?

HAVE A
A HAPPY
XMAS

Read very slowly the words in the panel.
What does it say? Are you sure?

8

What do you see—four arrows pointing to the center or a standard cross with a diagonal cross behind it?

Which looks bigger, the brim or the height
of Abraham Lincoln's top hat?

Rotate very slowly this page with the
hypnotic square. What do you see?

Is this a black circle with two leg shapes or is it something else?

Stare at this picture without blinking for about 30 seconds. Then look at a sheet of white paper. Who do you see?

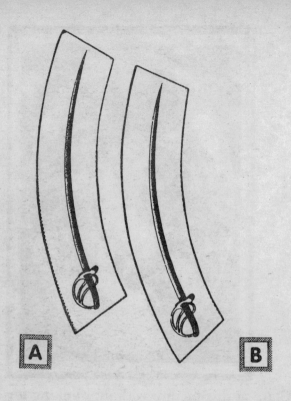

Which of these two sabers is the longer, A or B?

The sailor is looking through the telescope
to find his girlfriend. Can you find her?

This girl has a strange pet animal. Can you discover what it is?

What creature do you see here? Is it a
hawk or a goose?

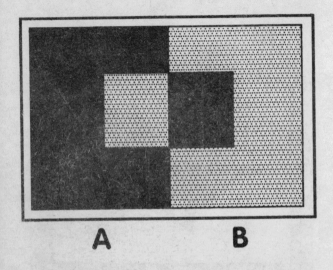

A   B

Are the gray areas the same shade? Which gray looks darker, A or B? Which looks lighter, A or B?

Can you see where Napoleon is hiding?

Stare at the center of this illustration and
then very slowly bring the page towards
your face. What happens next?

Is this a perfect circle?

Study this picture very carefully. Do you notice anything unusual?

This old design is called three faces under one hat. Can you guess why?

This lady went on a diet. Examine the picture very carefully. Can you see what she looked like at the end of her diet?

Can you figure out what this set of abstract symbols represents?

→ ←

Place a pencil along the line of the two arrows. What happens to the color of the wheel?

Can you see what's wrong with this poster?

What do you make of the design on page 29? To find out, tilt the page to eye level as in the sketch above. Look in the direction of both arrows. What do you see? (This sometimes works best with one eye closed.)

29

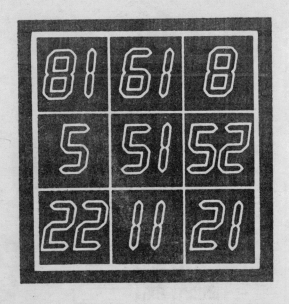

Every row of numbers in this square gives a different total. How can you make each horizontal, vertical, and diagonal line add up to give the same sum total?

Place two mirrors (without frames) at right angles to each other and look directly into them as shown. What happens?

What do you see? Two people looking at each other or a fancy vase?

Can you discover why this old British colonial patriotic design is called "The Glory of a Lion Is His Mane"?

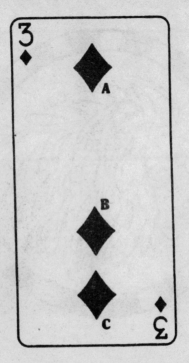

Carefully look at this playing card. Can you figure out which distance is greater, A–B or B–C?

Stare at this rabbit design without blinking
for about 30 seconds under a bright light.
Now look at a blank wall or a piece of
white paper. What do you see?

There are ten small variations in Picture "b."
Can you spot them?

36

Examine this bowl of fruit. Can you find the gardener?

This picture is based on a Victorian "Fantasy Face"–love of the clown. What do you see in this print?

These two boys are afraid of the giant, yet
he is hiding in the picture. Can you find
him?

TOO HOT TO HOOT

This phrase is known as a palindrome. It reads the same backwards and forwards. There is something unusual about it. Can you figure it out?

Which of these two bulls looks the larger?

Dobbin the horse has an animal
bodyguard. Which animal is it?

Keep staring at this design under a bright light. After a while, what do you see?

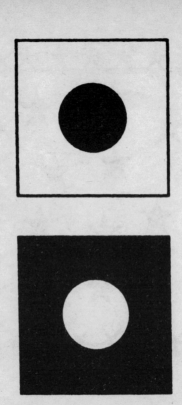

Which dot is the larger?

Can you unearth what these shapes represent?

Hold this page at arm's length. Now slowly bring the page towards your face. What happens to the two birds?

The girl has a thermometer in her mouth. Her temperature is 98.6. What is unusual about this number?

Does this picture frame get narrower as it gets towards the top?

Look at the girl on this swing. Which
looks longer, the upright or the horizontal
bar?

What do you see in this picture?

How many cubes are there in this sketch?

There are five mistakes on this playing
card. Can you see them?

Place the tips of your index fingers together and hold them just in front of your eyes. Now look just past your fingers and focus your eyes on something in the distance. Separate your fingers about half an inch. What do you see?

CHOICE DICE 50¢

The shop was selling poor-quality dice at 50¢ each. This was not the correct price. Can you work out what was the true price?

What do you see in this Victorian print?

This innocent-looking boy is very
mischievous. He has a cheeky pet animal
too. What is it?

Look at the intersections of the white lines.
What do you see?

Are these real circles?

Very slowly read the words on the front of the box. What does it say?

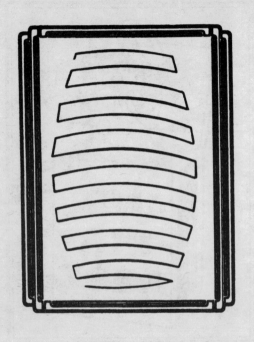

Using just your eyes, can you tell how many slats of wood there are on this barrel?

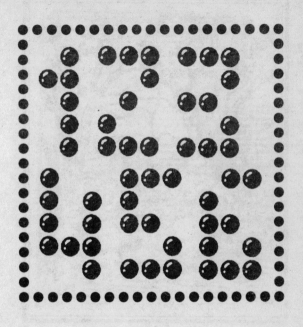

Can you decipher the meaning of these dots?

The soldiers are looking for the spy, but they can't find him. Can you?

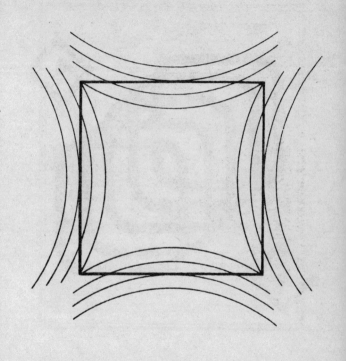

Is this a perfect square?

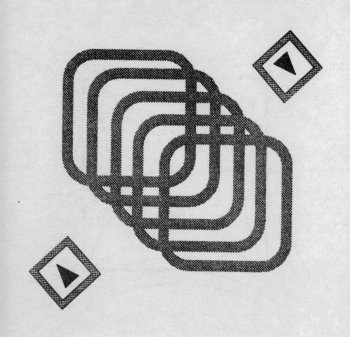

Is this set of squares pointing up to the left or down to the right?

Why is this picture called "The Lady of the Lake"?

What is the meaning of this set of letters?

Can you find this man's grandfather?

KID GLOVES
DICE GAMBLE
BEECH NUTS
CHOICE QUALITY
COOKBOOK PAGES

Turn this page upside down and look at its reflection in a mirror. What strange thing occurs when you do this?

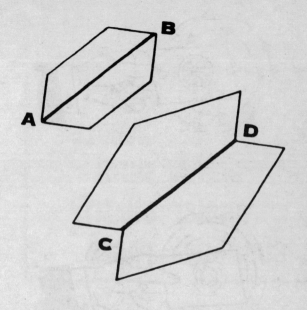

Which line is longer, A–B or C–D?

THE MAGIC SPINNER

Photocopy this page onto a piece of thin card. Cut it out and rotate it as shown on the opposite page. What do you see spinning in the disk?

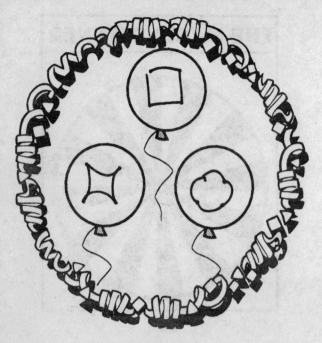

What will happen if you draw a square on a balloon with a ballpoint pen and then blow the balloon up? Can you figure out what the square will look like?

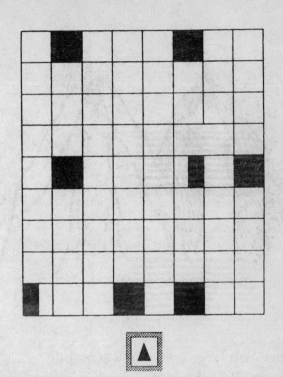

Can you discover this secret word?

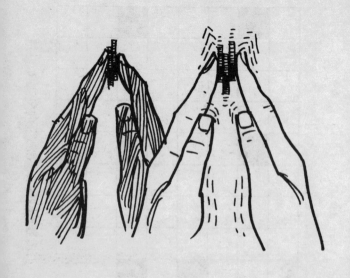

Place two large coins between your
fingers. Rub the coins together in a rapid,
short up and down motion. Look at the
coins and what do you see?

Observe this cow very carefully. Do you notice anything unusual about it?

The shepherd is playing his flute. Can you
find him hidden in this picture?

Can you work out what these shapes represent?

Put a bright postage stamp on the table and cover it with a glass of water. Now place a saucer on top of the glass. What happens to the stamp?

This man is sad because his daughter is about to get married and leave home. On the other hand, she is very happy. Can you find her?

This is a genuine postage stamp. If you turn it upside down and look carefully, you will discover another face. Who is it?

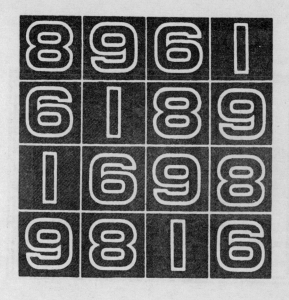

This is a "Magic Square." Each line—horizontal, vertical, and diagonal—adds up to 24. But there is another unusual thing about this square. Can you unearth the mystery?

How can you get the bird to fly into the
snake's mouth?

Is Side "a" of the illustration high or is
Side "b"?

Stare at this picture without blinking for about 30 seconds. Now turn your gaze onto a blank wall or sheet of white paper. A mystery figure will appear. Do you recognize him?

Can you work out what these shapes represent?

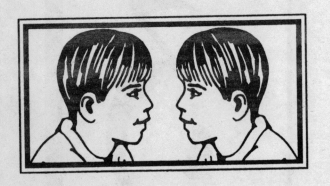

Try this experiment: Sit facing a friend. Slowly move towards each other until your noses almost touch. Keep staring straight ahead. What happens to your friend's eyes? Try it to find out, or try it on yourself by looking into a mirror.

86

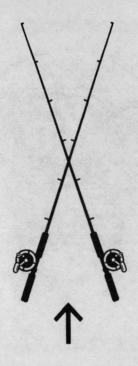

Hold the page at eye level and look at the fishing rods in the direction of the arrow. What happens?

Another design from times past. This British soldier is happy because the enemy is on the run. Who is the enemy?

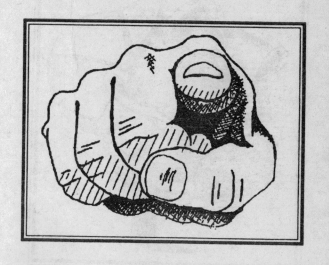

This finger is pointing straight at you.
Move your head from left to right. What
happens?

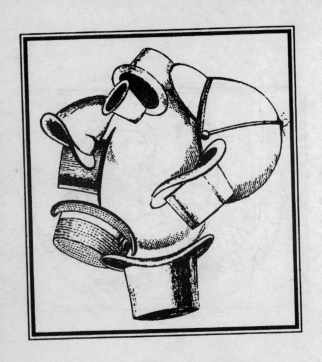

Here's a Victorian collection of different types of hat. Can you see anything else?

Which of these two dots is in the true center?

The illustration on page 93 is a copy of an
envelope posted in London in 1895. Hold
the card as shown. Can you find out who
the letter was addressed to? (This sometimes works best with one eye closed.)

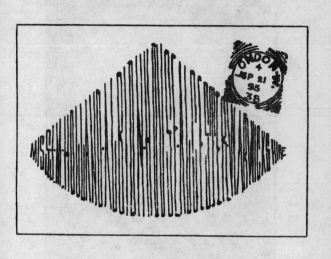

93

The original artwork for this print is called "Tête du Mort" (Head of Death). Why do you think it was given this title?

Bring the page slowly towards your face.
What happens?

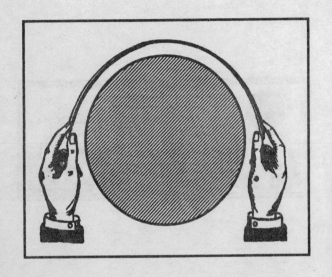

Stare at these diagonal lines for a while.
What do you see?

The farmer's son was adding up the large
number of eggs laid over a 3-week period.
Do you see anything unusual with the
answer?

Read the words on this notice board very slowly to yourself. What does it say?

Without blinking, stare at this portrait
under a bright light for about 30 seconds.
Now gaze at a piece of white paper or a
blank wall. Who do you see?

What is this creature, a rabbit or a duck?

Can you see what is unusual about this mysterious old lady?

Where is the master of this faithful horse?

Slowly rotate this page in a circular
motion. What happens to the clown's
balloon?

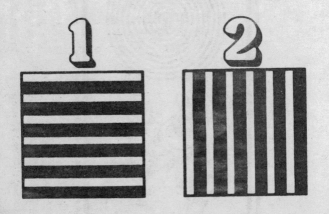

Which square is the wider and which one is the taller?

This design is made up from straight lines.
Look at it for a while and you may see
other shapes. What are they?

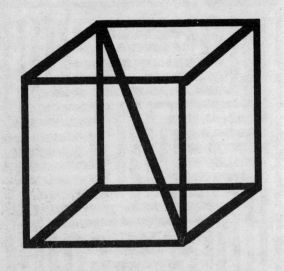

Are you looking down on this cube with
the diagonal line starting from the upper
left-hand corner, or are you looking up at
it with the diagonal line starting from the
lower right-hand corner?

In this woodland scene two giants are searching for a girl. Can you find all three in this picture?

Look carefully at the vertical threads the spiders have spun. Are the lines parallel, or do they bow in the middle?

The number 96 is not 69 upside down.
Can you explain?

Look at this frame very carefully. Does it
bulge out in the center?

Can you spot anything unusual about this bearded man?

Are you looking down a tunnel or are you on top of a pyramid looking downwards?

Can you find the man of the mountain?

Can you figure out the significance of the numbers beneath Napoleon's portrait?

How many children can you see in this vintage etching?

Without turning the book upside down, would you describe this man as happy or sad?

116

What animals do we have here, two ducks
or two rabbits?

How would you describe this illustration?
Is it a black square with four small white
squares inside, or is it four black arrows
pointing out to each corner?

This is another sketch from World War I.
Can you find the kaiser hiding in this tiger
design?

Can you find Santa Claus in this quaint
Christmas scene?

Look at the figure on the left. Is it sloping as in Picture 1, or does it slant as in Picture 2?

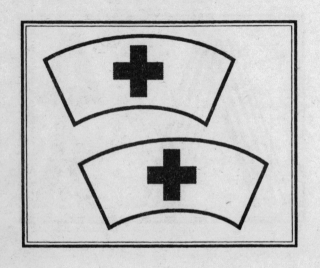

Which nurse's hat looks bigger?

Napoleon's supporters used to wear violets as a sign of their allegiance. This print hides the faces of Napoleon, Maria Louisa, and the young King of Rome. Can you find them?

What do you see, the head of a Native American or an Eskimo looking into a cave?

TOTI
EHORS
ESTO

The farmer posted this sign on his gate.
What was he trying to say?

Can you uncover the two secret messages
in the circle? Hold the page as in the small
sketch and look in the direction of the
arrows. This sometimes works best with
one eye closed.

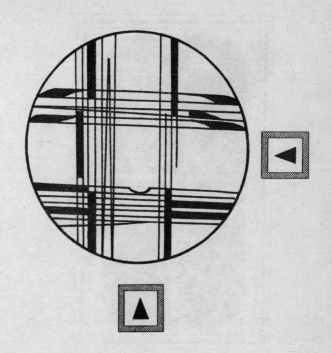

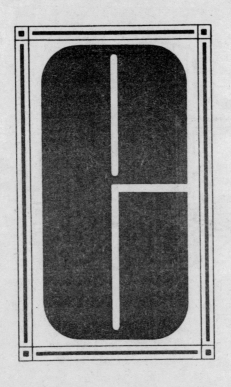

Do you recognize what the shape is?

This old sketch is called "Under the
Mistletoe." What's odd about the drawing?

What is the artist painting, a hunter or a tiger?

Are these five white stripes and six black stripes, or is it something else?

What do you see, white crosses on a black background or black crosses on a white background?

NO X IN NIXON

This phrase is known as a palindrome. It reads the same backwards and forwards. There is something else peculiar about the words. What is it?

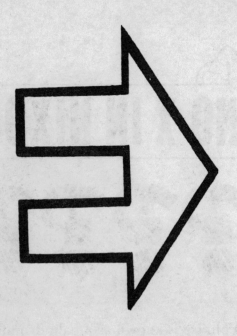

The shape is part of a sign we see in everyday life. Can you figure out what it is?

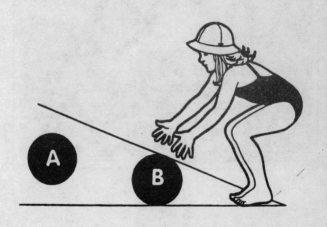

Which of these two beach balls looks
larger, A or B?

The mighty giant lives in the tower. Can you find him hidden in this print?

The elephant is weird. Can you guess
why?

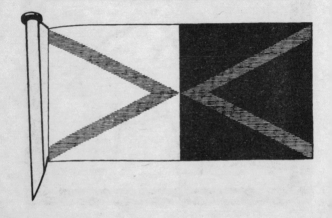

Is the cross the same shade in the two halves of this flag?

The clown is off to perform his show. Can
you find his puppets, Punch & Judy?

Hold the page about 3 inches in front of your face and gaze at the star and two clown hats. What happens?

What do you think this is?

Are the letters of this word straight?

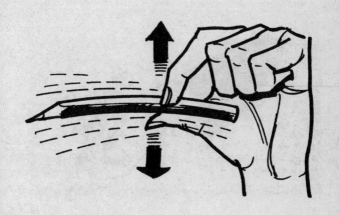

Hold a pencil between your thumb and
first finger loosely. Let it rock and wobble.
What appears to happen?

Can you guess the identity of these famous
people? Hold the book as shown and look
in the direction of the arrow. It sometimes
works best if you close one eye.

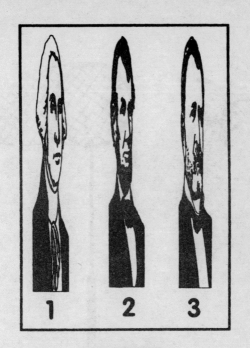

Slowly bring this page close to your face.
What happens to the butterfly?

This is another World War I picture. Rotate the page in a counterclockwise direction. What happens to the steam engine?

This person is sad. A visit to a circus
might make him happy. Can you find the
clown?

```
          W
        W A W
      W A S A W
    W A S I S A W
  W A S I T I S A W
W A S I T A T I S A W
W A S I T A C A T I S A W
W A S I T A T I S A W
  W A S I T I S A W
    W A S I S A W
      W A S A W
        W A W
          W
```

Study the letters carefully. How many times do you think it says, "Was it a cat I saw"? You can read it up, down, diagonally, etc.

This print is based on a Victorian design titled "Gossip" in which two ladies are in discussion. Look at the page from a distance and what do you see?

Can you find the hidden message? And is the answer yes or no?

Look at this postage stamp from different
angles and the face on the stamp will
change into an animal. What is it?

Place a small tube to your right eye. Now
hold your left palm towards you, against
the side of the tube. Both eyes must be
open. Now focus your vision on the
opposite side of the room. What happens?

153

Stare at this illustration without blinking for about 30 seconds. Now stare at a sheet of white paper or a blank wall. Who do you see?

154

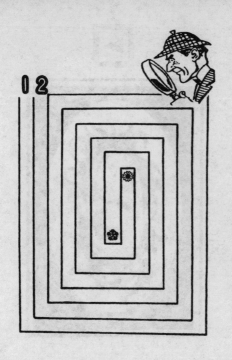

Using just your eyes, can you work out
which path leads to the black flower and
which leads to the white flower?

Can you figure out what this Victorian puzzle picture represents? Is it an animal, vegetable, or mineral? Look at it from different angles.

156

Photocopy this page onto a piece of thin
cardboard. Cut out the six pieces and
rearrange them to form a galloping horse.

Can you tell very quickly if Line 1 is longer or shorter than Line 2–3?

Hold this book in your right hand about 5 inches in front of you. Shut your right eye and look at the right-hand star. Bring the page slowly towards your face. What happens?

The solution to this mathematical problem is incorrect. How can you make right?

This old-time print shows a boy and his father. Can you find both of them?

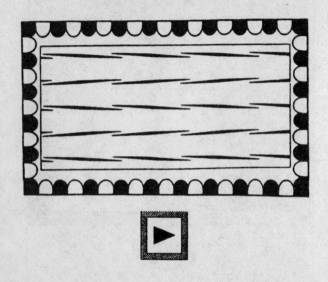

These horizontal stripes seem to be drawn
in a haphazard way. Hold the page at eye
level, close one eye, and look down at it in
the direction of the arrow. What happens?

Which rabbit in the hat looks larger, the black one or the white one?

The smoke signals say, "The food is tasty."
How do we know that?

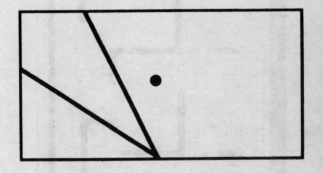

Copy this design onto a small piece of thin card. Spin the diagram on a pin. What happens?

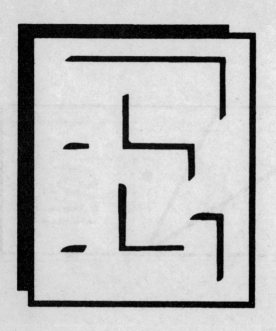

What do these shapes represent?

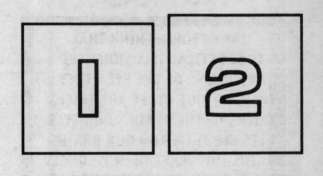

Which is the true square, Number 1 or 2?

MANY PEOPLE THINK THAT
THAT OPTICAL ILLUSIONS ARE
ARE TRICKS OF THE EYE - THEY
THEY ARE NOT - THEY ARE TRICKS
TRICKS OF THE BRAIN - OUR EYES
EYES SEE THEM AND OUR BRAINS
BRAINS INTERPRET THEM WRONGLY.

Can you spot anything unusual in this paragraph?

What creates the illusion of movement in this picture?

We read this passage as "dark cloud." Is the first letter a "c" or a "d"?

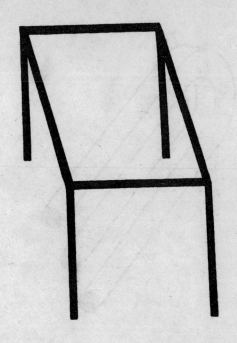

This is a curious table. Are you looking at
the table from above or below?

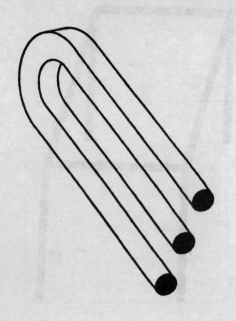

What is strange about this object?

This Victorian lady is unhappy because she went on vacation but the weather was cold. How did she look when the weather improved?

Two spies are hiding from the guards. Can you spot them?

Hold the page at eye level, close one eye, and look at the page in the direction of the arrows. Can you see yourself in the mirror?

Place a small mirror on the center line and look at the reflection in the mirror. What do you see?

Stare at this image for about 30 seconds without blinking. Now look at a blank wall or sheet of white paper. You will see the face of a well-known personality. Who is he?

There are two unusual things about this
word. Can you seen them?

This Victorian design is made up of a collection of boots and shoes. Do you notice anything else in this picture?

Can you decipher this strange sequence of symbols?

What do you see in this Victorian "Fantasy" face?

Hold this page at eye level, as shown in the sketch. You should see the name of a famous Victorian magazine. What is the name? (This sometimes works best with one eye closed.)

Which way do these bizarre numbers face, downward to the left or upward to the right?

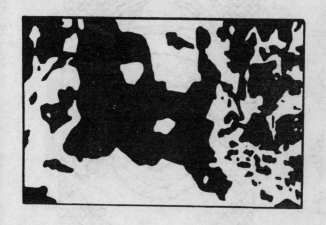

What can you uncover that is hidden in
this pattern of black and white shapes?

What is the occupation of this girl's father?

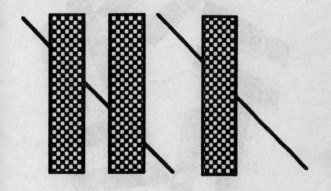

The diagonal lines are partly hidden by
the columns. Do you think they are
continuous lines, or are they disjointed?

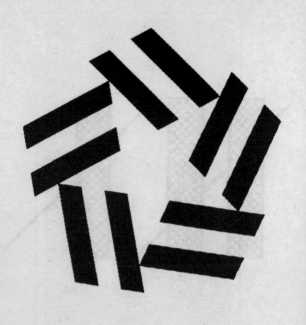

What do you see? Most people see ten dark lines, but there is something else. What is it?

This Victorian print shows an old lady and a young woman. Can you find both of them?

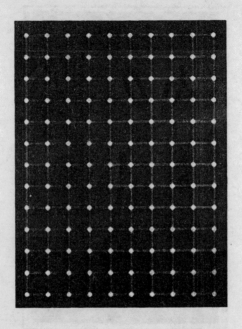

What do you see happening in the small
white circles at the intersections of the
lines?

Fold a small piece of cardboard in half and make it stand up on a table like the roof of a house. Now view it from above and the front. At first it appears normal, but stare at it for a while. What happens?

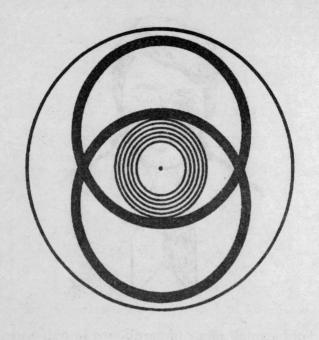

Make a copy of this disc and paste it onto
a piece of thin cardboard. Cut it out and
spin it slowly on a pin or nail. What
happens?

Look at the reflection of this page in a mirror. What happens to the words? Why do you think this happens?

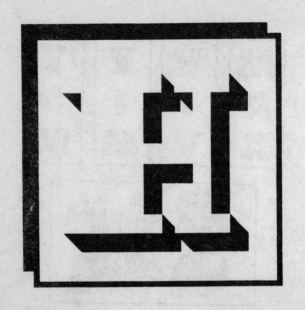

Can you make out what these shapes depict?

194

Les cercles parait
ront tourner si on
donne au dessin
un léger mouvement
de rotation.

Rotate the page slowly. What happens to
the piece of cord the clown is holding in
this old-time French print?

What do you see in this design? It can be
seen as two arrows or a letter of the
alphabet. What is the letter?

196

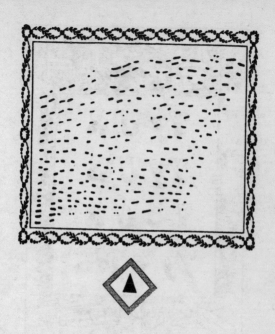

This picture looks like a haphazard
collection of small dashes, but if you hold
the page at eye level and look in the
direction of the arrow you will uncover a
word. What is it?

The sign writer has painted a series of
letters of the alphabet. Can you unravel
his secret message?

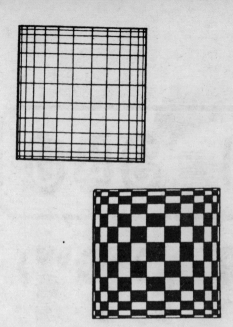

Look at the pattern in the top square. The square below is exactly the same design, but some of the squares have been filled in. How has this altered the appearance of the design?

This mathematical sum is wrong. What can you do so that it is correct?

Can you find the likenesses of
The Misses Frances & Grace Hoyt, Vocalists
who will appear here with

Sousa And His Band

Look at this old-time poster. Can you find
Frances and Grace?

FINEST
PICKLED
ONIONS

What's wrong with this picture?

The cavalier is looking for his opponent,
but he can't see him. Can you?

AREY
OUSCA
RED?

What do the words on this haunted house mean?

Using just your eyes, can you count how many squares are there in this design?

Study this snow scene. You will see an animal. What is it?

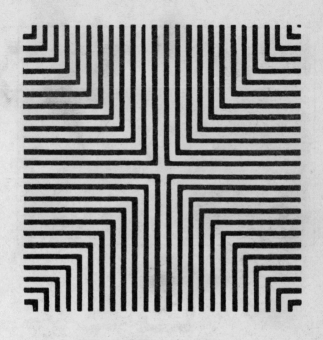

This item of "op art" is made up of
straight lines. Stare at it for a while and
what do you see?

This quaint Christmas scene conceals the face of Santa Claus. Where is he hiding?

The magician's assistant has been sawed in two halves. Can you think of a way of making her whole again?

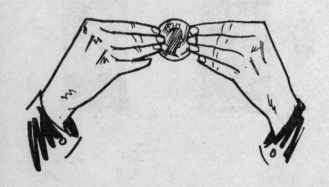

Put a large coin between your fingers and bring the hands together with a kneading motion. What appears to happen to the coin?

The proud peacock has a proud owner.
Can you see where he is?

Part of the shoe seems to be missing. What does our brain do?

A Mystery.

HOW MANY CUBES, 6 or 7?
COUNT THEM AGAIN!
DIFFERENT EACH TIME.

A STILL GREATER
MYSTERY
CARL HERTZ
The World-Famous
ILLUSIONIST.

This is the giveaway of illusionist Carl
Hertz. Do you see 6 or 7 cubes?

What do you see here, a young man or an old man?

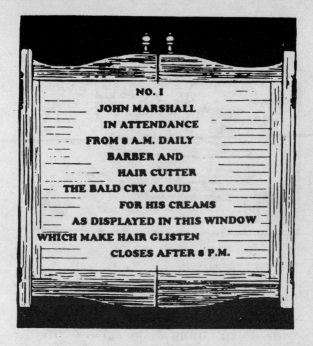

NO. I

JOHN MARSHALL

IN ATTENDANCE

FROM 8 A.M. DAILY

BARBER AND

HAIR CUTTER

THE BALD CRY ALOUD

FOR HIS CREAMS

AS DISPLAYED IN THIS WINDOW

WHICH MAKE HAIR GLISTEN

CLOSES AFTER 8 P.M.

On a very windy day this doorway created
a problem for John Marshall. Can you
unravel the mysterious thing that
happened?

Draw a top hat on a piece of round
cardboard. On the other side draw an
upside-down rabbit. Make small holes on
the edge and thread a piece of cord
through (see illustration). Hold the cord
with your fingers and twirl it around a few
times. What happens to the design?

Back to
to
School

What does it say on this chalkboard?

This was the personal number plate on the lion's truck. What's special about it?

Why do you think this illustration is called
"The Wedding Belle"?

This is a genuine postage stamp. It shows
Christopher Columbus discovering
America. The artist made a mistake in his
design. Can you see it?

Hold a small pocket mirror between your eyes so that you can look around both sides into a larger mirror. If you place the mirrors parallel to one another, what do you see?

Who is larger, Fritz or Paul? Try tracing one of them and measure it against the other.

Can you see both the boy and his father?

MAGIC HAS AN IRRESISTIBLE FASCINATION FOR CHILDREN OF ALL AGES. THERE IS NO FINER FORM OF ENTERTAINMENT THAN A PERFORMANCE OF MAGIC ... FULL OF FUN, FANTASY, MYSTERY AND LAUGHTER.

How many times does the letter "F" appear in the above paragraph?

Study this chess piece very carefully. What else can you see?

This jigsaw puzzle looks like a six-pointed star. Examine the design. Can you see anything else?

Can you figure out what this stained-glass
window shows?

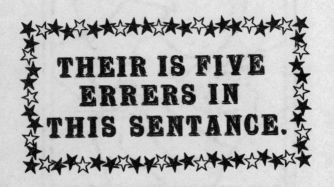

THEIR IS FIVE ERRERS IN THIS SENTANCE.

Read the words in the panel. Is the statement correct?

This is the poster of vaudeville performer T. Elder Hearn. He was a protean, or quick-change artist. What do you see in this publicity print?

Stare at this bulb under a bright light for
about 30 seconds. Now stare at a piece of
white paper. What do you see?

Lig Htupwit Hafla Shofins Pirati On!

What does this sequence of letters mean?

What do these shapes depict?

Copy this design onto a piece of thin
cardboard and pierce the center with a
pin. Now spin the disc like a top. What do
you see? Try spinning it clockwise, then
counterclockwise.

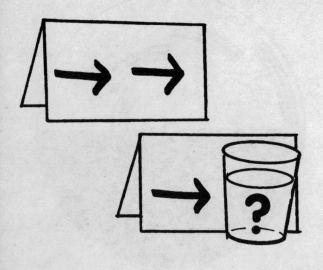

Draw two arrows pointing in the same direction on a thin piece of folded cardboard. Place an empty glass in front of one of the arrows. Now slowly fill the glass with water. What happens next?

Hold a piece of cardboard in front of your forehead and try to write your name. You will be surprised by the results. What happens?

What playing card is represented by this illustration?

Can you figure out the meaning of the pattern in the small frame?

This landscape design hides the face of the
farmer. Can you find him?

ici est le Portrait du Docteur Quitira

ha voila mon Portrait

This portrait was first published in Rome
in 1585. What's special about it?

Concealed somewhere in this old sketch is
the baker. Can you find where he is
hiding?

Stare at this figure for a time. What appears to happen?

Come over here.

Slowly bring this page closer to your face so that your nose almost touches the dot. What happens to the man and woman?

What does it say in the fortune-teller's ball?

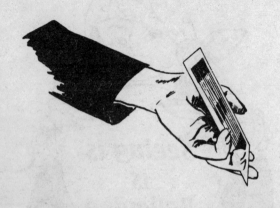

Hold the page as in the sketch and look in
the direction of the arrows. Five items will
be revealed, all relating to a famous
French magician from times past. Can you
discover them? (This sometimes works
best with one eye closed.)

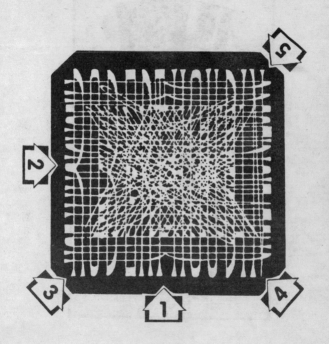

This is a Victorian portrait of a
grandfather. Can you see anything else?

Stare at this cameo print for about 30 seconds without blinking. Now look at a piece of white paper or a blank wall. Which famous person do you see?

Are these bricks in straight rows or have they been built in a haphazard way?

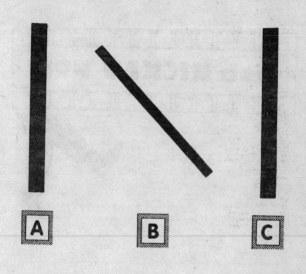

Does Line B look longer or shorter than Lines A and C?

bob KICKED PoP

Why did Bob kick Pop? Turn the page
upside down and look at the reflection of
the page in a mirror.

This is a series of blobs and blotches, yet our brains fill in the missing bits. What do we interpret them as?

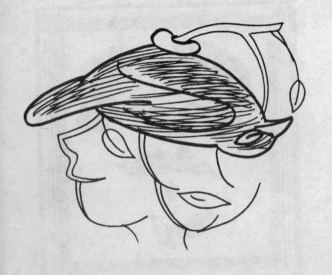

The young girl is full of the joys of spring.
She can hear a bird singing. Can you find
it?

Make a small dot on a piece of paper and place it on a table in front of you. Now try to touch the dot with a pencil held in the hand. This is easy, but what happens if you close one eye? Try it and see.

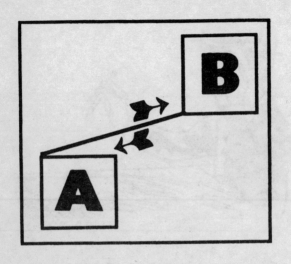

Is Square A at the front and Square B at the back, or do you see Square B at the front and Square A at the back?

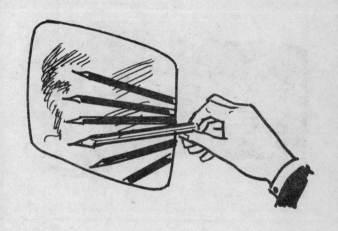

Wag a pencil in front of a television
picture. What appears to happen?

These unhappy villagers are crying
because they can't go to the dance. A
magician made their wish come true and
they were happy. Can you make this
group stop crying?

What is the artist drawing, a series of
numbers or a portrait of a business man?

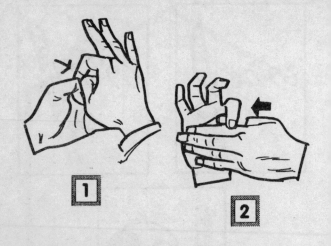

Hold your left hand out in front of you.
Point to the right, with the palm facing
you and the top of the thumb bent towards
you (Picture 1). Place your right thumb
against it as shown, with the right
forefinger covering up the joint. If you
slide your right hand along the left
forefinger, what appears to happen?

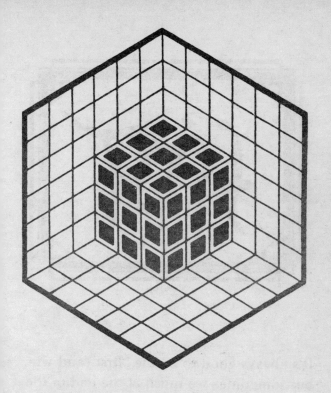

Is this a dark cube in a corner or is it a white cube with a corner cut away?

It's always good to be the "first" and win, but sometimes we finish at the end of the race. What word would you use and can you find it in this picture?

Can you figure out the message from these cryptic letters?

While the boys are playing around the
trees, the farmer is watching. Can you find
him?

Move the page slowly from left to right in the direction of the arrows. What happens to the center part of the picture?

Does this sign say "Knowledge" or does it say "Ignorance"?

264

Can you figure the meaning of this set of shapes?

Daisy the Cow is rather timid. The creature she hates most is a frog. Can you think of a way of transforming her into one?

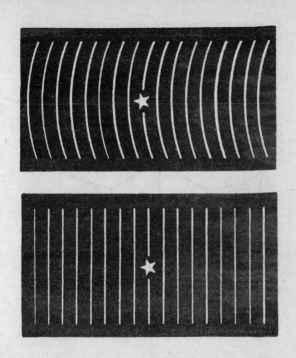

Look at the top drawing and focus your
attention on the center star while counting
up to 100. Now look at the bottom
drawing. What happens?

This large cheese had a piece cut out. Can you locate the missing portion?

268

What's wrong with these two boxes?

Seen from a distance, this picture looks like a man's head. What else do you see?

Can you work out what these shapes
represent?

Can you uncover what the farmer was trying to say in this message?

There is something very strange about the time displayed on this digital clock. What is it?

THE STATUE OF OF LIBERTY

Read the words on the panel. What do they say? Are you sure?

274

Can you find the old soldier?

Hold up one of your index fingers and
shut one eye. Now open and close
alternate eyes. What appears to happen to
your finger?

Is the top of the lamp shade longer than
the top of the lamp base?

There are four hidden messages in this
old-time advertisement for two of
London's famous magicians. Hold the
page as in the sketch and look in the
direction of the arrows. (This sometimes
works best with one eye closed.) What are
the phrases?

How can these four lines be arranged to make the number 10?

Stare at this black-and-white print for about 30 seconds without blinking. Now look at a sheet of white paper or a blank wall. Who do you see?

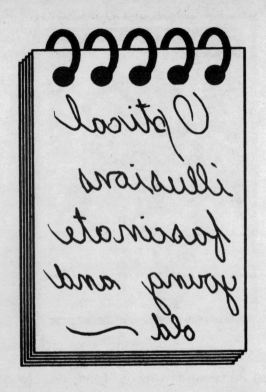

Reflect on this: How can you read this puzzling message?

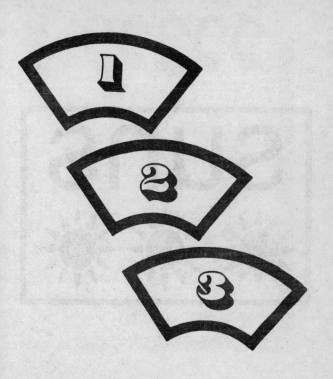

Which of these three boomerang shapes is
the largest?

Do you notice anything curious about the word "suns"?

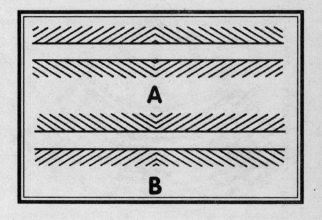

Do the horizontal lines "A" dip in the center and the lines "B" bulge in the center?

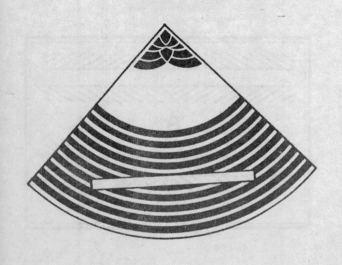

Does the small white strip rise in the center?

Magician Horace Goldin used this flyer to publicize his theater shows. Who looks taller, Goldin as a man or as a boy?

Place a jar over a coin lying on a table; it will look as though it is in the jar. Now fill the jar with water and put the lid on. What happens to the coin?

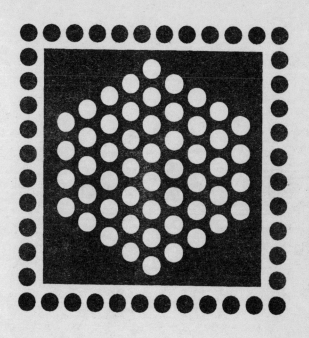

Stare at the white circles on this page.
What happens to them?

Slowly bring this page towards your face.
What happens to the boy holding the
bowling ball?

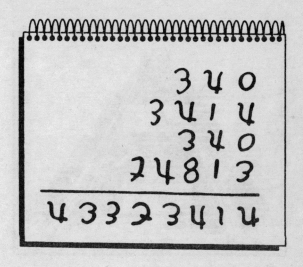

This mathematical problem does not add up correctly. How can you make it correct?

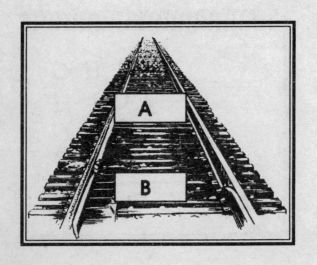

Which of the two rectangles looks longer, A or B?

Can you guess what this shape is?

As the scouts take a rest, the enemy is watching. Can you find the adversary?

Look through a jar filled with water. Stand
a pencil a foot behind it. The image
appears doubled in the jar. What happens
if you close your right eye? What happens
if you close your left eye?

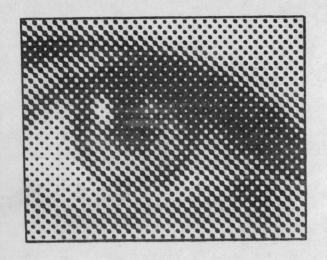

This series of black and white dots is an illusion found in newspapers every day. When seen close up, they are meaningless. What do you see when you view them from a distance?

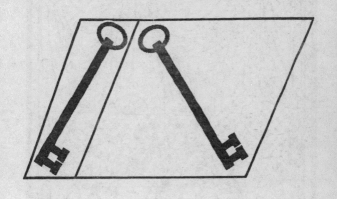

These two keys have been drawn in a
parallelogram. Is one bigger than another?

Can you find the performer? He is hidden in the design. Try looking at the picture from different angles.

298

Which is greater, the distance from 1 to 2 or 3 to 4?

Can you work out which word these arrows represent?

Stare at this illustration for about 30
seconds. Now look at a sheet of white
paper or a blank wall. Who do you see?

NE1410IS

Can you figure out the significance of this sequence of letters and numbers?

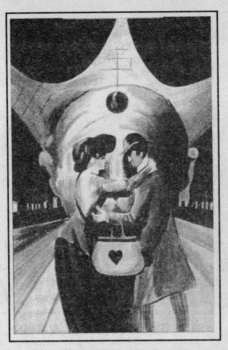

Look at this print close up and you will
see it is two people saying farewell. Now
view the page from a long distance. What
do you see?

This attractive landscape print holds a secret. Can you find the landlord?

What do you see here, three abstract shapes or a letter of the alphabet?

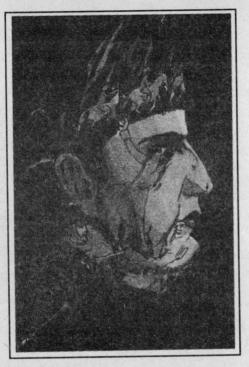

This print is based on a Victorian design. It shows the head of Napoleon. What else does it show?

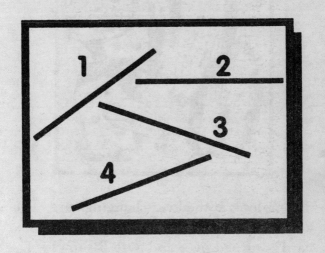

Using just your eyes, can you decide
which is the longest line?

Take a look at the ever-changing card. The audience sees Side A showing an ace. The card is turned over and Side B shows a 4. Turning the card back to Side A shows it has changed into a 3. Finally, turning the card back to Side B has now changed it into a 6. Can you guess how the trick has been done

Prick two small holes (no more than an eighth of an inch apart) in a piece of thin cardboard. With one eye, look through the two holes. Hold a pin about an inch away on the other side. What happens to the pin?

This symbol is used as a sign for recycling. What is it though—a black arrow on a white background or a white arrow on a black background?

What do you see, three abstract shapes or an object?

It's very easy to make hand shadows. All you need are your two hands and a bright light. An easy one to make is a dog's head. Can you guess what following Drawings 1 and 2 will make? Try the experiment with your own hands.

312

SHADOWS

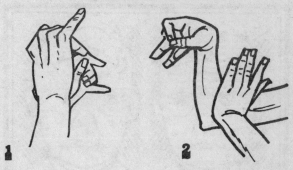

1   **2**

Now that you're an expert at hand
shadows, can you work out what two
shadows will be created when the hands
are placed as shown?

The twins are sad because they have reached the end of this book. How can you make them happy? There are two solutions.

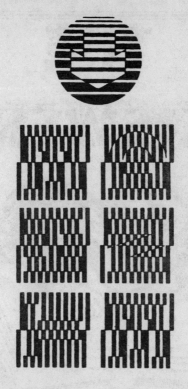

This "op art" series of panels contains a
secret message. Can you decipher it?

THE ANSWERS

Page 6. Both mouths are identical. The arrows at the end of the lines confuse us.

Page 7. It reads the same when turned upside down.

Page 8. It says "Have a a Happy Xmas."

Page 9. It depends on how you look at it. Both answers are correct.

Page 10. They are both the same size.

Page 11. It appears to spin.

Page 12. The letter "S."

Page 13. George Washington.

Page 14. They are both the same size. It's the curve that confuses us.

Page 15. Turn the picture upside down. You will see her head wearing a bonnet.

Page 16. Turn the page upside down. Her pet is a pig.

Page 17. It depends on how you look at it. Both answers are correct.

Page 18. They are both the same shade.

Page 19. His head is shown by the "X." See below.

Page 20. The woman places the flower in the man's buttonhole.

Page 21. Yes, the background lines confuse us.

Page 22. The boys are sitting on an impossible staircase. Study the picture. The top stair becomes the middle stair, and vice versa.

Page 23. There are two side profile faces looking at each other. When combined they form a third face that is looking straight ahead.

Page 24. Concentrate on the left-hand side of the picture, starting with her face. You will see a thin lady.

Page 25. It's the letter "G."

Page 26. Although it is the same shade of gray, the part over the white area appears to be darker.

Page 27. Look at the sequence of words. It says "the with." It should be "with the."

Page 29. 1. Shakespeare. 2. He was not for an age but for all time.

Page 30. Turn it upside down. It will then become a "Magic Square" with each row adding up to the number 45.

Page 31. You'll see yourself as others see you. Wink your right eye and see what happens.

Page 32. It all depends on how you look at it.

Page 33. Look at the lion's mane. You will see some of the old British colonies: Canada, India, Australia, New Zealand, and African colonies.

Page 34. Both distances are identical.

Page 35. A white rabbit in a black hat. That's magic!

Page 36. Here are the ten differences: Rabbit's right ear, left eyelash missing, nose filled in, part of right whisker missing, line under right eye missing, right hand is different, two lines under chin missing, line missing from right foot, left thumb is missing, dots under nose missing.

Page 37. Turn the page upside down, and there he is.

Page 38. The print is of two Pierrot clowns. View the page from a distance and watch it change into a gruesome skull.

Page 39. Turn the page upside down. One of the boys is climbing on his beard.

Page 40. It also reads if you look at its reflection in a mirror.

Page 41. Both bulls are identical in size.

Page 42. A dog. Turn the page upside down. The dog can be seen tied up to a tree.

Page 43. You see flashing white stars bouncing among the black stars. Try to focus on these "afterimages" and they will vanish.

Page 44. Both dots are the same size, but lighter objects look bigger than darker ones.

Page 45. The letter "E."

Page 46. The birds go into the cage.

Page 47. It reads the same when turned upside down.

Page 48. No, it doesn't. The sides are parallel all the way to the top. The pattern confuses us.

Page 49. Both lines are the same length. The upright line appears to look longer.

Page 50. Is it an old-fashioned telephone or a picture of two dogs looking at each other? It's both. It all depends on how you look at it.

Page 51. It can be 3, or if you look at the center of the picture you may see an extra one—making a total of 4.

Page 52. 1. The corner numbers are in the wrong corners. 2. The lower number 2 has been reversed. 3. The pip under the reversed number 2 is upside down. 4. The central top and bottom pips should go in opposite directions. 5. There are 3 central pips; there should only be 2.

Page 53. You will see a floating sausage, the size of which depends on how close or how far apart your fingers are. See illustration at the right.

Page 54. Turn the page upside down. Now look at its reflection in a mirror and you will see the correct price is only 20¢.

Page 55. Another macabre picture. Viewed close up, it's a young lady looking at her reflection in a mirror. Viewed from a distance, it's a grinning skull.

Page 56. A monkey. Just turn the page upside down.

Page 57. Flashing gray dots.

Page 58. Yes. To prove it, trace round one of them with a compass.

Page 59. It says "Jack in a a box."

Page 60. There is only one. It's a single continuous line.

Page 61. The numbers 1, 2, 3, 4, 5, 6. Viewing the page from a distance helps.

Page 62. Turn the page upside down. You will see his face formed from the branches.

Page 63. Yes. This is another illusion where the background lines fool us.

Page 64. Either is correct. It all depends on your viewpoint.

Page 65. The arrangement of tree, birds, and boat reminds us of a face.

Page 66. A wise one foresees seasons.

Page 67. Turn the page upside down.

Page 68. The word "COOKBOOK" and those

beneath it all read correctly because the letters used to make the words all have horizontal symmetry.

Page 69. Both lines are the same size.

Page 71. You will see a ghostly image of a small silver/gray coin. The size of the coin depends on the size of the rotation.

Page 72. The square gets larger but generally retains the same shape. The lines will get wider.

Page 73. The secret word is "LAUGH." Look at the page at eye level in the direction of the arrow.

Page 74. The ghostly image of a coin appears sandwiched between the two coins you are rubbing.

Page 75. Look at the markings on the cow's back. You will see a map of the United Kingdom.

Page 76. See illustration at the right.

Page 77. It's the word "THE."

Page 78. It disappears. Look at it from all angles. It's gone—just another one of those strange illusions.

Page 79. Turn the page upside down.

Page 80. It looks like an old Asian man. Daniel Webster's shirt forms his forehead.

Page 81. It also works if you turn the image upside down.

Page 82. Hold the page at eye level and slowly bring it towards your face. The snake swallows the bird.

Page 83. It all depends on your viewpoint.

Page 84. General Ulysses Grant.

Page 85. The number 6.

Page 86. Your friend will appear to have one eye in the middle of his or her forehead.

Page 87. You will see an extra rod. Sometimes you may see two extra rods. Amazing!

Page 88. The kaiser. Many of these types were issued during World War I.

Page 89. It appears to follow you, but it's just an illusion.

Page 90. From a distance it looks like a man's head.

Page 91. The one that is on the line, although it

looks like the other one.

Page 93. Miss S.I.M. Holland, Albion House, Alcester, Warwickshire.

Page 94. Close up we see a couple of people on a sled. From a distance, it's another of those grinning skulls that were popular in the Victorian era in Europe.

Page 95. You should see 3 balls and 5 glasses. Experiment with different distances.

Page 96. Many people see impressions of very pale colors.

Page 97. Turn the page upside down and it says "Lots o'eggs."

Page 98. It says, "This house is for for sale."

Page 99. Abraham Lincoln.

Page 100. It all depends on your viewpoint. This ambiguous picture "flip-flops."

Page 101. Turn the page upside down. She looks exactly the same.

Page 102. Turn the page upside down to find him.

Page 103. The balloon starts to appear to spin.

Page 104. Both squares are identical. The one with horizontal stripes should appear to be wider. The one with vertical stripes should look taller.

Page 105. You will probably see a small diamond shape in the center of the design surrounded by a bigger diamond shape.

Page 106. You can see this any way you want.

Page 107. Turn the page upside down. The two giants are looking down at the girl.

Page 108. They are parallel. It's the web in the background that confuses us.

Page 109. Turn the number 96 upside down, and it still shows 96.

Page 110. No, it doesn't. The sides are parallel. The design on the frame tricks us.

Page 111. Look at his face. It shows a postman with a sack of mail.

Page 112. Either one is correct. Keep looking at it and it will change.

Page 113. Turn the page so that the arrow points in an upwards direction. The man of the mountain will make his appearance.

Page 114. Look at the reflection of this page in a mirror. The numbers will change into the word "Emperor," which was Napoleon's title.

Page 115. Initially we see 3. But since each head can join onto the different bodies, we get a grand total of 7. Can you work it out?

Page 116. At first glance we assume he's happy, but really he's sad. We are not used to seeing faces upside down. Since the mouth and eyes have been inverted, he seems very weird when we look at him.

Page 117. Either, they are whatever you want them to be.

Page 118. It's both, but most people see the white squares first.

Page 119. Turn the page so that the arrows point upwards. Look above the tiger's eyes and you will see the kaiser looking to the left.

Page 120. Turn the page so that the arrow points downwards. You will see Santa's face. The building in the center forms his nose.

Page 121. The design "flip flops." Take your pick!

Page 122. They are both the same size. Trace one of them and measure it against the other.

Page 123. "X" marks their spot. See illustration at the left.

Page 124. Either is correct. The decision is yours.

Page 125. To tie horses too.

Page 127. The messages are: 1. How is. 2. your Dad.

Page 128. It's a letter "e."

Page 129. The face can belong to the man or the woman.

Page 130. This is another ambiguous picture. It's both things at the same time.

Page 131. It's a letter "B."

328

Page 132. The choice is yours.

Page 133. You can still read it if you turn the page upside down.

Page 134. See illustration at the right.

Page 135. They are identical. Ball "B" should look larger.

Page 136. Turn the page so that the arrow points downwards. You see the giant.

Page 137. This elephant is made up from the letters E L E P H A N T.

Page 138. Yes. The one against the darker background appears to be lighter.

Page 139. Punch can be seen if you look at his jacket. Judy can be seen behind his right trouser leg; where the knee bends becomes her nose.

Page 140. You will see three hats and two stars.

Page 141. It's a letter "E" from a typeface called "Antique Extended," which was designed in 1840.

Page 142. The letters are perfectly upright. The background pattern confuses us.

Page 143. The pencil will appear to bend and look as though it were made of soft rubber.

Page 145. They are: 1. George Washington, 2. Abraham Lincoln, 3. Ulysses Grant.

Page 146. It flies into the net.

Page 147. The steam engine goes backwards.

Page 148. Turn the page upside down.

Page 149. According to puzzle expert Sam Lloyd, there are 63,504 ways!

Page 150. You will see a grinning demon.

Page 151. The message, made up from white letters, is "Can you find the words."

Page 152. Turn the stamp upside down and the face looks like a monkey in a hat.

Page 153. It appears as though there is a hole in your hand.

Page 154. Charlie Chaplin.

Page 155. No. 1 leads to the black flower, No. 2 to the white.

Page 156. It is a dog curled up on a rug. Turn the pages so that the arrow points downward.

Page 157. See illustration below.

Page 158. Both lines are the same length.

Page 159. The left-hand star disappears.

Page 160. Turn the page upside down. It now reads X = 1 + 1X. This is mathematically correct.

Page 161. Most people see the boy. You do not have to turn the page upside down to find the father. The boy's chin becomes the father's nose. It may help if you look at the page from a distance.

Page 162. They appear to be candy-stripe poles.

Page 163. Both are the same size, but the lighter rabbit appears larger than the darker one.

Page 164. Turn the picture upside down and you will see a man licking his lips.

Page 165. You will see two concentric circles.

Page 166. A letter "E."

Page 167. Number 2.

Page 168. The last word in every line appears twice.

Page 169. The extra lines around the second clock create the illusion of movement.

Page 170. It's both. It depends on what you read first—the horizontal or vertical word.

Page 171. The table can be seen in both views. It flip-flops.

Page 172. It is impossible to make. The legs are an illusion that can only be drawn.

Page 173. Turn the page upside down.

Page 174. If you turn the page upside down, you will see the two bearded spies.

Page 175. You will see a donkey! Try this trick on your friends.

Page 176. It will still read HEIDI. This works because the letters have horizontal symmetry.

Page 177. John F. Kennedy.

Page 178. It reads the same backwards and forward.

It also reads the same upside down.

Page 179. A bizarre face.

Page 180. It says "July Illumination" with its reflected image.

Page 181. Close up it's two women and a child. From a distance, it's a soldier.

Page 183. The Strand Magazine.

Page 184. The letters flip-flop, so that we can see them pointing down to the left or up to the right.

Page 185. A bearded man's head. See illustration at the right.

Page 186. He's a sailor. Turn the picture upside down.

Page 187. The lines are continuous.

Page 188. A star is formed in the center of the design.

Page 189. The young lady's chin becomes the nose of the old lady. View the page from a distance.

Page 190. Black dots will start flashing on and off.

Page 191. It will appear to reverse, and stand on end like an open book.

Page 192. It looks like a pair of black circles whirling around a white one.

Page 193. The names are still legible. This happens because the letters used have vertical symmetry.

Page 194. The letter "H."

Page 195. The cord looks as though it is spinning around.

Page 196. The letter "H."

Page 197. The word "Projection."

Page 198. It says, "Too wise you are
          Too wise you be
          I see you are
          Too wise for me."

Page 199. It takes on a curved appearance.

Page 200. Turn this page upside down. It now says, "One = 1."

Page 201. Turn the page upside down. You will see the two profile faces of the sisters.

Page 202. The onions are too large to enter the neck of the bottle.

Page 203. Turn the page upside down and he will be revealed.

Page 204. It says, "Are you scared?"

Page 205. Thirty.

Page 206. A Dalmatian dog.

Page 207. It will change into 4 triangle shapes.

Page 208. Turn the page so that the arrow points upwards. Santa's face will be revealed.

Page 209. Bring the page close to your face. She will join up as if by magic!

Page 210. It will appear to be flexible and look as though it is bending.

Page 211. He is found by turning the page upside down.

Page 212. Our brain fills in the missing bits, and we perceive it as a shoe. This is an example of a "closure." Look at pages 25, 45, and 85 for other examples of this type of illusion.

Page 213. It all depends on your viewpoint.

Page 214. It can be either of the two suggestions. The choice is yours.

Page 215. The left-hand door swung open leaving the right-hand side still in position. Cover the left-hand side of the door with a piece of blank paper and read the new message.

Page 216. The rabbit will look as though it is sitting inside the hat. See illustration below.

Page 217. It says, "Back to to School."

Page 218. By turning the page upside down, the plate changes into "Leo Lion."

Page 219. The two figures form the outline of a bell.

Page 220. This stamp issued in 1903 shows Columbus holding a telescope, which had not yet been invented.

Page 221. You will see an unending series of mirrors that stretch into the distance.

Page 222. They are both amazingly the same size!

Page 223. Turn the page upside down.

Page 224. There are 12 letter "F"s in the paragraph.

Page 225. Look carefully and you will see two profile faces.

Page 226. It can also be seen as three cubes.

Page 227. A boy blowing a bugle. See illustration at the right.

Page 228. The sentence should read, "There are four errors in this sentence." But since there are in fact five errors, the word "four" should have been replaced by the word "five."

Page 229. A part of his act is shown close up. From a distance, it resembles the performer, T. Elder Hearn.

Page 230. You will see a lighted bulb.

Page 231. It says, "Light up with a flash of inspiration."

Page 232. The word "Eye." Focus your attention on the white areas of the shapes.

Page 233. You will see colors appear from nowhere. The colors vary according to whether the design is spun clockwise or counterclockwise.

Page 234. The arrow points in the opposite direction.

Page 235. Your name is in mirror writing.

Page 236. The three of hearts (Tree of Hearts).

Page 237. The message says "Easy if you read between the spots."

Page 238. Turn the page 90° clockwise, and you will see him.

Page 239. If you turn the page upside down, Doctor Quilira changes into a donkey.

Page 240. See illustration at the right.

Page 241. The rays will appear to pulse and vibrate.

Page 242. They will hold hands.

Page 243. It says "Seeing is is Believing."

Page 245. All the words are about the French magician Robert Houdin, who was born in 1805 and is regarded as the father of modern-day magic: 1. Robert Houdin, 2. Prestidigitateur (French for "magician"), 3. St. Blois (place near where he was born), 4. Physicien, 5. Mecanicien.

Page 246. His eyes and mustache are made from two young girls.

Page 247. Thomas Jefferson.

Page 248. They are in straight rows. Place a ruler on them to check.

Page 249. All three lines are the same length.

Page 250. Because Pop kicked Bob.

Page 251. We recognize these shapes as a bearded man's head.

Page 252. Turn the page upside down.

Page 253. In most cases you will miss the target. It's difficult to estimate distance with just one eye.

Page 254. It can be whatever you want it to be.

Page 255. You will see many separate outlines of a moving pencil.

Page 256. Turn the page upside down.

Page 257. Take your pick.

Page 258. It will appear as though you are removing the tip of your thumb.

Page 259. Either answer is correct.

Page 260. Turn the page upside down and the word will change into "last."

Page 261. Captain Forbes (4 B's)

Sent his forces (4 C's)

To the West Indies (West in letter D's).

Page 262. Turn the page 90° counterclockwise.

Page 263. The central disc will appear to float.

Page 264. The choice is yours.

Page 265. A face looking up.

Page 266. Turn the page upside down.

Page 267. The lines will curve in the opposite direction.

Page 268. Turn the page upside down and you will find the missing piece.

Page 269. They are impossible to construct them.

Page 270. You will see two people facing each other.

Page 271. The letter "G."

Page 272. It reads "To tie a goat to."

Page 273. It's a palindrome. It reads the same backwards and forwards. It also works if you turn the page upside down.

Page 274. It says "The Statue of of Liberty."

Page 275. Turn the page 90° counterclockwise.

Page 276. Your finger will appear to jump.

Page 277. They are both the same length.

Page 279. It reads: 1. Maskelyne and Devant, 2. St. George's Hall, 3. Home of Mystery, 4. Daily at 3 and 8 London.

Page 280. Cover up the top and bottom of the illustration with your hands and you will see the number 10.

Page 281. Ronald Reagan.

Page 282. Look at the page in a mirror. Do you agree with the message?

Page 283. They are all the same size.

Page 284. It reads the same upside down.

Page 285. It's just an illusion. Both sets of lines are parallel.

Page 286. No, it is perfectly straight. The background lines confuse us.

Page 287. They are both the same height.

Page 288. It will look as though it vanished.

Page 289. They will look like hexagons.

Page 290. He will go towards the pins.

Page 291. Turn the page upside down and it will be mathematically correct.

Page 292. They are both the same size, although A should appear longer.

Page 293. The number 3.

Page 294. Turn the page 90° counterclockwise.

Page 295. If you close your right eye, the left-hand pencil disappears. Close your left eye and the right-hand side pencil disappears.

Page 296. An eye.

Page 297. Both keys are identical in size.

Page 298. See illustration at the right.

Page 299. They are both the same distance.

Page 300. The word is "news"; the arrows are pointing North, East, West, and South.

Page 301. A bearded man.

Page 302. It says "Anyone for tennis."

Page 303. A clown wearing a three-pointed hat.

Page 304. Turn the page 90° counterclockwise. His face will appear.

Page 305. It's the letter "Z."

Page 306. You will see a battle scene with people on horses, etc.

Page 307. Line 3 is the longest.

Page 308. See illustration at the right. This shows how the card is made. Just draw some spots on the two sides of a card with a marker. By placing your fingers in the different positions the card appears to have changed, but it's just an illusion.

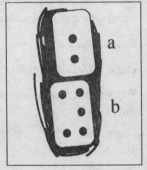

Page 309. You will see two pins.

Page 310. It's another one of those designs that can be interpreted either way.

Page 311. It's a square frame with a small block at its center. Looking at the picture from a distance sometimes helps.

Page 312. A rabbit. See illustration at the right.

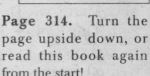

Page 313. The shadows are of a man and a swan. See illustrations below.

Page 314. Turn the page upside down, or read this book again from the start!

Page 315. Turn the page so that the arrow points to the left. You will be able to see the words "The End."

ACKNOWLEDGEMENTS

The author wishes to thank the following for contributing materials and offering advice: Edwin Dann, Dr. E.A. Dawes, Arthur Day, Dr. J. Ergatoudis, T. Edward Hordern, Clifford Hough, Brian Lead, Max Matthews, Denny Plowman, George Pott, Tim Rowatt, Jacqueline Wills, with special thanks to the staff at Bolton Central Library for research help. I would also like to thank Roy Litherland again for all his help in proofreading.

As with the first volume, I have spent a lot of time and effort researching in order to make the data furnished as correct as possible. Unfortunately, in a number of cases I received no reply to my inquiries. The author/publisher would be pleased to hear of any discrepancies so that any errors can be rectified.

With some of the older material, the originator is not known. Some of it has been published many times without mention of the artist, so it has been impossible to give credit where credit is due.

Index